VERMONT
HERITAGE

VERMONT

Montpelier, near the center of the state,
On *Onion River*, rules o'er small and great.
  Windsor upon *Connecticut* may reign,
  As Burlington is found on *Lake Champlain*,
  And *Otter Creek* has fair Vergennes' upon her,
Known for the *fleet* of Commodore McDonough;
  And Mid-dle-bu-ry on this tide may tarry,
Known for her *college* and her *marble quarry*.
  And Bennington, southwest of all, we mark
Famed for the victory of General Stark.
— George Van Waters, 1849

Vermont Heritage

A PICTURE STORY

BY Barrows Mussey

AUTHOR OF *OLD NEW ENGLAND*

ILLUSTRATED WITH OVER 170 OLD ENGRAVINGS
FROM *The Museum Society*, BRATTLEBORO, VT.

A. A. Wyn INC.: NEW YORK MCMXLVII

Pictorial assistant, Ruth Mary Canedy, Jacksonville, Vermont

It is a pleasure to acknowledge the help of State Senator F. Elliott Barber, Jr., of Windham County; Fenton Batton of Brattleboro; the staff of the Brattleboro Public Library; Alfred W. Bushnell of Brattleboro; Jason E. Bushnell of Vernon; W. D. Canedy of Jacksonville; John E. Clark and the Tuttle Company, of Rutland; Donald B. Cram of Keene, N.H.; A. Luke J. Crispe of Newfane; A. D. Faber of New York; Robert Kolvoord of the Old Settler Bookshop, and Eric Lundberg, both in Walpole, N.H.; Gerald McDonald and the New York Public Library; Walter Needham of Guilford; and Doris E. Robbins of Brattleboro.

The illustration of Leland & Gray Seminary was most generously furnished from the private collection of F. Cabot Holbrook, Brattleboro.

Printed in the United States of America

Composition by
E. L. Hildreth & Company
Brattleboro, Vermont

Contents

THE STATE IN 1824

Green Mountain Country

Few of the visitors to Vermont, and by no means all the people who live there, have any idea of the rich heritage behind those dreamy valleys and busy little towns. Vermont from the outside may look like a picturesque region that welcomes vacationists, and tries to put the clock back on election day — the last home of ox teams, maple syrup, and quaint individualists. But if the state is no more than this, why has it not fallen apart, like some other eastern states, into mill towns on the one hand, vacation playground on the other?

The answer lies in the country, in the people, and ultimately in the heritage that these pages attempt to trace.

R. L. Duffus (who should know, for he comes from Burlington) once called Vermont a "social museum." The secret of Vermont is its vitality: the museum is alive and thrifty. The old ways persist here because on the whole they still meet our needs. The settlers whom you see above on their way to establish the Connecticut River settlements at Vernon, Fort Dummer, and Westminster would be surprised, no doubt, to see Vermont now — but not, on the whole, displeased. Vermont still lives in a way that these pioneers could have understood. Life in the Green Mountains is not easy, and never will be; but pleasant and rewarding it is.

7

It is pretty well agreed that the first permanent white settlement within the present boundaries of Vermont took place in Vernon, the southeasternmost town. Northfield, Massachusetts, was settled in 1673; and at some uncertain time afterward, Massachusetts settlers built Bridgeman's Fort, which you see at the left.

Then in 1724 Fort Dummer was built, south of modern Brattleboro. The first commander of Fort Dummer was Captain Timothy Dwight, whose son was probably the first white child born in Vermont territory, and in turn the father of the great Timothy Dwight, president of Yale and Congregational "pope of Connecticut."

Considering his father's birthplace, it was a little unkind in President Dwight to say of the Vermont pioneers, "These men cannot live in regular society. They are too idle; too talkative; too passionate; too prodigal; and too shiftless; to acquire either property or character. . . . Under the pressure of poverty, the fear of a gaol, and consciousness of public contempt, they leave their native places, and betake themselves to the wilderness.

"The second proprietor," he admits, "is commonly a *farmer;* and with an industry and spirit, deserving no small commendation, changes the desert into a fruitful field."

Sartwell's Fort (right) was another of the Connecticut Valley blockhouses, built in 1740. Although comparatively Vermont had little trouble with the Indians, these early forts suffered repeated attacks; the first Bridgeman's Fort was destroyed in 1747, and had to be rebuilt afterward.

Brattleboro, on the Connecticut River, is the chief town of Windham County, which has always belonged more to Dwight's farmers than to his pioneers. The settlers came largely from Connecticut, "the land of steady habits"; they soon grew solid and prosperous. The people in Windham County stuck to the churches and the ways they had been brought up in; they were not restless and pushing like the Champlain "foresters."

Before Vermont was a state — or even a royal province — the Green Mountains belonged to New York. But since no one from New York did anything about it, Governor Benning Wentworth of New Hampshire began selling off grants in the wild west across the Connecticut. Perhaps the Windham County towns preferred the more distant authority; they backed New York, some of them even after Vermont declared itself an independent state.

Yet Brattleboro has never refused to welcome what it thought a good idea. In 1845, before the United States issued postage stamps, the Brattleboro postmaster made his own.

The eastern and western slopes of the Green Mountains have always been different. They looked different, and the people acted differently. One reason was that you could go more easily from Windsor, say, all the way down into Massachusetts than half the

distance west, across the mountains. Traveling through ice, mud, and rocks was terribly hard work. The first steamboats on the Connecticut, just before 1830, gave way to pole- and sail-propelled flatboats, which brought Putney, for instance, closer to Connecticut than to northern Vermont. And finally the railroads, which began running in 1848, even hurdled the mountains. Eastern and western Vermont still differ, but not so glaringly; the railroads have brought them together, whereas the waterways drew them apart.

OLD MILL
PUTNEY

OPERATED CONTINUOUSLY
UNTIL 1946

The pretty village of Westminster is among the oldest in the state, and has a turbulent history that you would never guess to look at its single long, peaceful street now. In the battle between infant Vermont and New York, much of the actual fighting went on here. At the left, above, is the old courthouse, built in 1772. Around it took place the Westminster "massacre" of 1775, when a party of Revolutionary Whigs barricaded themselves inside. The New York high sheriff and his Tory followers routed the Whigs out, killing three in the process.

Next to the courthouse is a picture of John Norton's tavern, which was Tory headquarters during the disturbances.

Below is the thriving village of Bellows Falls, a paper making center where the very first bridge across the Connecticut stood.

Bellows Falls has grown and changed with the times since it first took its name from Colonel Benjamin Bellows of Walpole, across the river in New Hampshire. But if you go back up the slope of the mountains to such places as Townshend (above), you find villages that would still seem like home to their doughty settlers. In Townshend, for instance, lived General Samuel Fletcher, who fought in the French and Indian wars, at Bunker Hill, at Ticonderoga, where he commanded a company of Minutemen, and at Bennington. He was later high sheriff of Windham County.

When Townshend Green was first cleared, you could not drive an ox cart across it without tipping over; but by the time our picture was made, just before the Civil War, it was a smooth lawn surrounded by neat white buildings, as it is today.

At the right is the old West-minster meeting house. Vermont declared itself independent at Westminster, and the first printing within the present borders of the state was done here in 1778 by Judah Paddock Spooner and Timothy Green, from New London, Connecticut. (And see Norwich, page 21.)

13

Now we are going over the mountains. As I have already hinted (but it cannot be said too often), before the railroads came you could cross the mountains not at all in spring, and only with difficulty in summer and fall. In winter you could do it, unless you froze to death in the attempt. This was the fate that you see overtaking a Mrs. Blake, who set out by sleigh with her husband and baby across the mountains at the southern end of the state in 1827. They were lost in a blizzard; Mr. Blake set out to find help. He failed. Meanwhile his wife wrapped the baby in most of her clothes, with the result that she was found dead in the morning, but the baby was alive.

Lorenzo Dow, a roving Methodist preacher, told of his December ride to Brattleboro: "In the name of God, I set out in the hard snow storm. The snow had fallen about knee high, so that the mountains were almost impassable by reason of snow, steepness, mud and logs; the people thought my life would be endangered by the falling of trees, or the extreme cold in the woods, as there was no house for several miles, and the wind blew exceeding hard. I frequently was obliged to alight and stamp a path for my horse."

The mail (right) went through much more regularly in winter by sleigh than it could at any other season.

14

From historic Bennington Ethan Allen first defied New York, and the Revolutionary battle won by General John Stark on August 16, 1777, started Burgoyne's downfall. Actually the battleground (shown below) lies in New York; but Green Mountain Boys did all the fighting.

Old Bennington now is a show-place; at first it too was wild west. Said a traveling missionary in 1789, "Capital at present of Vermont — a good town of land, people, proud — scornful — conceited & somewhat polished." "The Meeting house makes but a mean appearance and is disgraceful to the place," adds an observer of 1797. He cannot have meant the one at the right. Perhaps his complaint brought the new building.

To save trouble, let us imagine ourselves already back across the
mountains to Weathersfield, just south of Windsor. Mount Ascutney
dominates the landscape, which is perhaps as varied as that of any
town in Vermont. At Weathersfield Bow, in one corner, William
Jarvis took the lead in the Merino sheep-breeding for which Vermont
was once famous; Perkinsville, in another corner, grew up as a mill
village, but a pleasant one; from Greenbush, in yet a third corner,
came Isaac Eddy, the engraver whose prints are now among the
choicest (if certainly not the most skilful) rarities sought by col-
lectors. The slopes of Ascutney, in addition to harboring limestone
and soapstone quarries, were long a happy hunting ground for geolo-
gists.

Not far from Greenbush, in the town of Reading, stand the
"Indian stones" that you see at the top of the next page. They mark
a step in the captivity of the Johnson family, who were carried off
from Charlestown, N.H., to Canada by the Indians in 1754. The
How family, carried off from Vernon in 1755, and Zadock Steele
(Royalton, 1780) were the chief Vermont Indian captives.

Mrs. Johnson's narrative of their sufferings was among the most famous of all the popular "Indian Captivity" books. Long afterward she herself, as a very old woman, put up the slate markers half a mile down the brook from the spot where, somewhat apart from her captors, she was delivered of a daughter, Elizabeth Captive Johnson.

No single picture could do justice to the peculiar genius of Springfield — a great manufacturing center jammed into a gorge of the Black River sometimes not ten feet across, yet not a mill town in the ordinary dismal sense. For its size, modern Springfield undoubtedly produces more machine tools (the tools that make tools) than any town in the world, yet it still looks like a Vermont village. It has never had either a railroad or river transportation.

In the days when Merino sheep were the chief glory of Vermont, Springfield was a textile town. A man from New Hampshire in 1808 started a cotton mill, a woolen mill, a carding shop, an oil mill, and a foundry. The town has bustled ever since. About the middle of the nineteenth century there were even efforts to grow silkworms.

Wooden dolls came a little later; if you can find a Springfield doll at an antique shop, you may think yourself lucky. Machine tools invaded the town from Windsor, just up the Connecticut Valley, in the 1890s, when shops still looked a bit like this. By now they have remade it. Springfield has produced a great crop of ingenious Yankee inventors and industrialists.

17

At the left is a church in Woodstock, belonging to a sect that grew up of its own accord in Vermont, though other branches started a little earlier in the south and west. Dr. Abner Jones of Lyndon withdrew from the Baptist Church in 1801, saying he pinned his faith on the Bible alone, and rejected any label except that of a Christian. And so this is simply a Christian Church (often pronounced Christi-an by way of distinguishing it from its neighbors).

Woodstock has always been one of the prettiest and most inconspicuously opulent towns in Vermont, and it still is. Memories of Woodstock Green have gone with travelers and missionaries to the four corners of the earth; a picture by a Japanese artist a century ago showed an unmistakable Green with Japanese foliage and houses. Our view below is even more lifelike; you will recognize it if you have been lucky enough to visit Woodstock.

The town is more than a showplace, too — shire town of Windsor County, and the home of several active printers and publishers in the past 140 years. One weekly was the *Universalist Watchman*, *Green Mountain Evangelist*, *Impartialist*, *and Christian Repository*.

Perhaps the parking problem in Woodstock was even more acute with a truly automotive rig like this one, requiring a hitching post, than it is now. Although this was less than a hundred years after the town was founded, it had already grown sedate and civilized. The early inhabitants, says a historian, "suffered much by the ravages of the wild beasts. In order to preserve their young cattle and sheep from the bears and wolves, they were, for some years, compelled to guard them during the night, or shut them up in yards, or buildings, prepared for the purpose."

Among the famous men whose accomplishments go to make up the heritage of Woodstock were Jacob Collamer, Zachary Taylor's Postmaster General; George P. Marsh, a linguist, scientist, and diplomat, perhaps unrivaled among the sons of Vermont; and Hiram Powers, once world famous as the sculptor of *The Greek Slave*, who was born in the house at the right, later the oldest in Woodstock. His grandfather, Dr. Stephen Powers, was one of the first settlers. Hiram's portrait is on page 37. He made his name abroad, but Woodstock did not forget him.

It is astonishing what a large share of Vermont towns have kept their antique, back-country charm. I believe, as I said before, that this is because the old charm goes deeper than clapboards and grass roots. The old life is still being lived, with what improvements gasoline and electricity have added. Furthermore, automobiles seem to have brought the old and the new ways closer together again, undoing some of the effects once produced by the railroads. Cars combine locomotive power and riverboat smoothness.

I thought it kinder, therefore, to show you one of the few places where the railroad *does* run through the countryside like a rusty nail through wood, not as it is now, but as it looked a quarter century after traffic was opened. The first passenger train in Vermont ran from White River (below) to Bethel in 1848. As late as the 1870's, though, the whole scene was "one of quiet beauty." "It needs but a glance to indicate that we are in the midst of the mountains. We can almost feel the invigorating breezes. We could easily throw down the burden of life's cares, and give up ourselves to the romance of the place."

Norwich, the very next town north of White River, needs no such indulgence. Every visitor (as well as every resident) must make up his own mind which among the many fine towns of Windsor County is the handsomest. Certainly Norwich, with its green plain, brick houses, and hills in the background, is a strong contender.

The view shows bits of Dartmouth College, at Hanover, N.H., in the distance. For a little while during 1778 and 1779 Dartmouth declared itself in "Dresden, Vermont," and the same men who did the first printing at Westminster printed before this at Dresden. The present New Hampshire towns of Cornish, Lebanon, Lyme, Orford, Piermont, Haverhill, Bath, Lyman, Littleton, Dalton, Enfield, Canaan, Orange, Landaff, Lisbon, and Franconia also joined themselves to Vermont during that brief period, when the quarrel with New York was boiling briskly.

Norwich University (page 43) was founded here, but moved to Northfield in 1866. A hereditary feud with Dartmouth was thus broken up.

The stagecoach will carry us once more across the mountains; the railroad to Woodstock is gone.

Rutland and Burlington are probably the only two places in Vermont with the nature as well as the name of cities. Above we see Rutland in 1860, already twice the size it had been in 1800. Sixteen years before that, it was not even the county seat of its own county. And for a brief burst about 1880, marble quarrying and railroads made it bigger than Burlington, which had been twice as big in 1850, and is more than half again as big now.

An English traveler in 1808, coming into Rutland after sunset, "found the public curiosity engaged by a sitting in the courthouse, on some persons apprehended on a charge of counterfeiting bankbills. As this was an offense of which I had heard much in all parts of Vermont, I had my curiosity too, and I repaired immediately to the tribunal. I saw, through the dusk, about a hundred persons, shabbily dressed, standing, sitting, and reclining on the benches and tables. I descried, upon the bench, four or five men, dressed like the rest, but bare-headed, while all the others wore their hats. Jury there was none; the single prisoner present sat, undistinguished, among the lookers-on. By degrees, I discovered, that though there was a whole bench of judges, and six or eight lawyers at the bar, this honourable court consisted only in one of the magistrates, his bareheaded companions being but assistants in courtesy."

The prisoner was put "under bonds" for fifteen hundred dollars, the whole random proceeding having been simply to decide whether there was enough evidence to make it worth while committing him for trial.

Schooling has been hard to come by in Vermont, and correspondingly prized. You could always count on the early artists to make pictures of academies, even though they might ignore the towns that housed them. On the right, for instance, is Troy Conference Academy at Poultney. The Methodist Church founded it in 1836. A Methodist historian ob-

served, "Perhaps there is no institution of the professed grade of this, which ranks higher in literary merit, or any whose location promises better security to the health and morals of youth. The scenery around is such as will please the taste, and improve the intellect." But the Academy, not the scenery, appears in the picture. At all events he was evidently right, for the building is now part of Green Mountain Junior College, and has been a school continuously for more than a hundred years.

Horace Greeley learned the printing trade at East Poultney.

Castleton, the next town to the north, is full of fine old houses, but again the school is what made the impression. In 1818 Drs. Selah Gridley and Theodore Woodward started a course of medical lectures, the origin of the Castleton Medical College. With one interruption the college pursued its founders' "design that country students shall not be compelled to resort to the cities, at an increased pecuniary expenditure, and the exposure of health and morals," until 1854. Once connected with Middlebury, it was finally joined to the University of Vermont.

The building is now part of Castleton Normal School (and incidentally Vermont had the first normal school in the United States, a model for all others, founded at Concord Corner in 1823 by the Reverend Samuel Reed Hall, who also wrote the first American textbook on teaching).

23

Going north again, we come to Hubbardton. Here is the scene of the only Revolutionary battle actually fought on Vermont soil. Like Bunker Hill, it was a British victory, but so dearly bought that Colonel Seth Warner and his Green Mountain troops accomplished their mission of protecting General St. Clair's retreat. One Vermont writer, twenty years after the event, laid the defeat "to the conduct of General *St. Clair*, who is so well known for his *innumerable retreats*, and for being *always* defeated." At all events the routed Colonials reassembled in time to help General Stark win the Battle of Bennington.

Still heading north, we come upon Brandon, once famous for its bog iron deposits and the Conant stoves cast from the iron. Obviously the men below are mining the iron, some of which lay a hundred feet down, though most of it was near the surface.

Two famous sons of Brandon were Stephen A. Douglas, "the little Giant" (page 38), Lincoln's great adversary before the Civil War, and Thomas Davenport, the blacksmith who invented the electric motor in 1837, and built the first streetcar.

The Brandon Baptist Church was built five years before Davenport invented his motor, but nineteen years after Stephen Douglas was born next door. Conant had been making his stoves, the first in Vermont, for a year or two by then. The bed of bog iron ore, said a gazetteer, was "inexhaustible," and made "the best of stoves," small cannon, and bar iron. Brandon also afforded manganese and some of the early Vermont marble quarries.

The picture of the Lake Dunmore House in Salisbury goes back to 1855, the beginning of an industry that has flourished soundly in Vermont without running wild — the resort trade. Tourist travel had started even earlier.

The picture was "drawn expressly by a lady artist, who prepared her sketches on the spot. A very large number of visitors last season went up to Lake Dunmore from this city," said the Boston editor, "and we have not seen a single person who was not enraptured at the beauties of the spot. Artists were and are there sketching the delightful features."

If the summer visitors have not had time to "spoil" Vermont since 1855, they probably never will.

When anyone says Middlebury, he is pretty sure to be thinking of the college (page 42). School and town have been tied together since 1800, when the college was chartered; but the first graduating class, in 1802, consisted of a man named Aaron Petty. Before the college had grown enough to carry weight, Vermont marble quarrying began. The first quarries of consequence that the state had were at Middlebury; they produced not only stone but an abundance of mechanical inventions — the modern method of sawing marble with sand and water (used in classical antiquity, and then forgotten); the first door- and sash-making machinery; the welding of cast steel.

The college was just struggling to its feet, too, partly under the influence of the hard-traveling President Timothy Dwight of Yale, when Emma Hart Willard arrived. She was a great teacher, a pioneer in female education, and the author of *Rocked in the Cradle of the Deep;* she went from Middlebury to New York State, where she started a school that is still eminent throughout the country.

The first settlement of Canadian French in Vermont was at Chimney Point, in the town of Addison, in 1730; it did not last as well as later ones, for they left in 1759. Chimney Point took its name from the gaunt ruins which were all that remained to tell the tale.

Montpelier owes its present eminence as capital of the state to compromise. The seat of government shuttled among Windsor, Rutland, and Bennington, with west and east sides of the mountains trying to land it, until in 1808 Montpelier, near the center of the state, became the permanent capital. One condition of its establishment was that a state house must be built. Montpelier met this requirement with the odd wooden building at the left. Of course it was heated by

stoves and lit only by candles. The assembly hall filled the bottom two stories; its straight, unpainted pine benches "were such a temptation to the ever handy Yankee jack-knife that in twenty-five years they were literally whittled into uselessness."

Whether from whittling or from state pride, Vermont decided in 1832 that it needed a new state house. The marble structure below, the showplace of the town, was finished in 1838. A fire gutted the building in 1857, but left the imposing front, which still distinguishes the enlarged state house of the present day.

Before 1800 "a circulating library of about 200 volumes of well selected books was established, in which most of the inhabitants became proprietors. To this may be attributed, in a good degree, the more than ordinary intelligence and taste for reading which has distinguished the inhabitants, especially the farming class of this town."

St. JOHNSBURY HOUSE.

The pleasant town of St. Johnsbury has in its time been known for four things — its name, unique in the world (after St. Jean de Crèvecœur, the French-American writer); platform scales, developed in their modern form by Thaddeus Fairbanks in 1830; missionaries; and the neighboring scenery. Willoughby Lake, reached by way of St. Johnsbury, rivaled Lake Dunmore for summer visitors as early as the 1850's.

At the right you see a freak inundation near Glover in 1810. Long Lake originally flowed off toward Lake Champlain. Less than a mile away was a much lower lake that flowed toward Memphremagog. Turning Long Lake eastward to feed the mills on Barton River proved a mistake, for this devastating flood instantly resulted.

SMUGGLER'S NOTCH
MOUNT MANSFIELD

This picture shows how completely Vermont and Burlington have been one in the public mind for almost a century past. At the first census, in 1791, Burlington was far to the rear even in Chittenden County — smaller than Charlotte, Essex, Hinesburg, Jericho, Shelburne, and Williston.

A minister from Connecticut two years before had observed crisply, "Colchester & Burlington all deists & proper heathen." But by 1810 it was the largest town in the county, and by 1840 the largest in the state. Ten years later it was still "Burlington village, not surpassed in beauty of location by any town or village in New England. A large share of the business on lake Champlain centres at this place, and the town is rapidly increasing in wealth and consequence," said a local historian. The steamer *Vermont*, on Champlain, was the second in the world to start regular commercial operations, in 1808. Lake steamers made Burlington for a time one of the world's great lumber ports.

"St. Albans village is a very flourishing place, containing a handsome park thirty by thirty-five rods in extent," said the geographer who printed this picture in 1860. Henry Ward Beecher was more emphatic: "A place in the midst of a greater variety of scenic beauty than any other I can remember in America."

St. Albans has enjoyed, apparently quite heartily, a turbulent past. Up through the War of 1812 smuggling to and from Canada was the leading industry. In 1814, eighty St. Albans volunteers set off on their own hook to help win the Battle of Plattsburg, which their less active fellow-townspeople watched anxiously from the hills across the lake. The most northerly bloodshed of the Civil War was the Confederate raid on St. Albans in 1864, when twenty-two Confederate soldiers robbed all the banks, killed a man, and fled into Canada with $200,000. Two years later a group of Irish revolutionaries called the Fenians started out from St. Albans to conquer Canada, but retreated peaceably after a six-mile advance.

Below is the railroad depot, depicted in an age when this was a source of pride. St. Albans has, as a matter of fact, done credit to its modern name of Railroad City. The industry that has nourished the town since 1850 has not at the same time made it hideous.

Green Mountain Boys

Two of the most famous events in Vermont history took place, oddly enough, in New York. We have already surveyed the Bennington battleground. And above is Colonel Ethan Allen with his eighty-five Green Mountain Boys, seizing Fort Ticonderoga at the southern end of Champlain in 1775. All the old history books have him demanding surrender "in the name of the great Jehovah and the Continental Congress," and our picture fits those ringing words better than the other versions offered by skeptical historians.

Surprising fifty sleepy Englishmen in the dead of night was not a hard road to glory; but it put the whole region under patriot control, and the captured ordnance and gunpowder were a rare prize for the Revolutionists.

It is not at all fair to write the history of Vermont around Ethan Allen, who merely led one of the groups that built up the state; but he was much the most picturesque of them all, the most profitable to his friends (his underlying interest in Vermont was real estate), the most horrifying to his enemies. He came up from Connecticut in order to make his fortune in the Onion River Land Company. He dearly loved a fight. He scandalized all respectable churchgoers with a pamphlet, *Reason the Only Oracle of Man*, much of it apparently lifted from his better educated friend Thomas Young. If you don't give him the stage, he takes it.

Allen was born at Litchfield, Conn., in 1738. Before 1770 he moved to Bennington, and then further and further up the west side of the "New Hampshire Grants" (which legally never belonged to New Hampshire, though Allen gave much energy to upholding its claim against New York) until old age caught up with him at Burlington, where he died in 1789, two years before Vermont joined the American union as the fourteenth state.

ETHAN ALLEN.

Next to Ticonderoga, Allen is remembered for his fight against the "Yorkites." Anyone who displeased him, and particularly New York surveyors and landowners, was liable to be roughly handled. Allen and his henchmen — his brother Ira, their cousins Remember Baker and Seth Warner, Peleg Sunderland — often treated these interlopers to the Beech Seal, as they called floggings like the one being administered to the unfortunate victim below.

The Allen brothers cared first and foremost about Vermont, which included their own property; everything else was secondary. Vermont had imitated the other colonies in declaring itself independent of Great Britain in January, 1777; Ethan Allen was quite ready for it to be independent also of the United States. Anything to keep New York land speculators from meddling with land-owning Vermont

patriots. It was the quarrel with New York that delayed independent Vermont in joining the Union. We notice that two years after Allen's death sufficed to settle a dispute of some forty years' standing. The trade of northwestern Vermont went more naturally to Montreal than to southward; Allen actually dealt with the British late in the Revolution, perhaps seriously, perhaps to hurry the Union and New York into meeting his terms.

General John Stark of New Hampshire (1728–1822), at the left above, won the Battle of Bennington. His "We beat them today, or Molly Stark's a widow" is almost as famous as Allen's Great Jehovah (and, I fear, just as likely never to have been said).

Green Mountain Boys fought for both heroes. The schoolbook of 1832 that printed the picture above said, "In the War of the Revolution, the soldiers of Vermont acquired great distinction for bravery; and the designation of Green Mountain Boys, which they bore, has ever been regarded as a title of renown. The following picture represents a company of these celebrated troops."

While Vermont was independent of even such a theoretical force as the Federal Union, it issued coins like the copper below, which was minted by Reuben Harmon, Jr., of Rupert. All money was so scarce, however, that Vermont had already passed a law allowing people to pay their debts with meat or grain.

The Rev. Nathan Perkins, a Connecticut Congregationalist, recorded in 1789, "Arrived at *Onion-river falls* & passed by Ethan Allyn's grave. An awful Infidel, one of y^e wickedest men y^t ever walked this guilty globe. I stopped & looked at his grave with a pious horror." The spot is at the right.

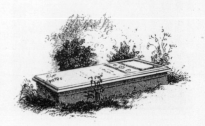

Above are two great men in early Vermont who, if not quite so picturesque as Ethan Allen, were more solid and stable citizens. Royall Tyler (1758–1826), at the left, "was a wit, a poet, and a chief justice" of the Vermont Supreme Court. In Guilford he wrote *The Algerine Captive*, the first American novel to be reprinted in England; this was but one of his brilliant writings.

At the right is Stephen Row Bradley (1754–1830), who moved from his native Connecticut to Westminster, Vermont, during the Revolution. He was by far the leading pillar of society in that region, and took a prominent part in Vermont operations to put down the New York party that centered around Guilford. He too was a member of the State Supreme Court.

Commodore Mac-Donough's victory in 1814 was off Plattsburg, N.Y., but his fleet had been built from standing trees to floating ships in 40 days at Vergennes, and many Vermonters helped him save the Green Mountains from British occupation.

35

"Vermont is a good State to be born in and a good State to go away from," said Stephen A. Douglas. Vermont has probably contributed a larger share of her people to the settling of the West than any other state. The rocky soil and steep hillsides would keep only a few of the early Vermonters' many children. Vermont suffered more than most of the states from the War of 1812, and the West began to look good. Then came "eighteen hundred and froze-to-death." On June 8, 1816, several inches of snow fell. There were no crops at all that year.

The family above are emigrants of 1817. They and many like them sought the promised land in western New York, Ohio, Michigan, Wisconsin. So it happened that leading men all over the country were born in Vermont. Some, like Brigham Young, left as children with their parents; others, like Jim Fisk and Thaddeus Stevens, struck out for themselves; there were even a few, such as John Godfrey Saxe and the exiled Henry Stevens, who still called Vermont home. So far as I know, they all took pride in their birthplace.

The Green Mountains have not lagged behind other parts of New England in producing scholars, and even prodigies. At the right, with playthings appropriate to his age rather than his learning, is Zerah Colburn, the mathematical wizard. He was born at Cabot in 1804; before he was six he could multiply 13 by 97 instantly; at eight he extracted cube roots. Traveling around with his father, he made a national sensation, and even did well in England during the War of 1812.

Truman H. Safford, Jr., of Royalton (born 1836), was a very similar prodigy.

Famous Men from Vermont

HIRAM POWERS (1805–1873), in his day the most famous American sculptor. Born in Woodstock; went by way of a waxworks museum in Cincinnati to world fame and an Italian studio in Florence.

JOHN GODFREY SAXE (1816–1887), born in Highgate, stayed in Vermont to edit a Burlington newspaper, and became the state's most celebrated writer of light verse, some of it still remembered.

JOSEPH SMITH (1805–1844), founder of Mormonism. Born at Sharon, he moved as a child with his parents to western New York, where he founded the Church of Jesus Christ of Latter-Day Saints.

BRIGHAM YOUNG (1801–1877), the successor to Joseph Smith as leader of the Mormons. He also moved as a child to western New York from his birthplace in Whitingham, on the southern edge of the state.

ALVIN ADAMS (1804–1877) started the Adams Express Company, a great carrying and banking concern that flourished until World War I, and merged with the Railway Express. He was born in Andover.

JAMES FISK JR. (1834–1872), born in Pownal, a tin-peddler out of Brattleboro, then a robber baron in the scandalous Erie ring along with Jay Gould. His murder was a sensation of the seventies.

THADDEUS STEVENS (1792–1868), born in Danville, leader of the radical abolitionists in Congress during the Civil War, creator of the 14th Amendment. He also launched the attempt to impeach President Johnson.

STEPHEN A. DOUGLAS (1813–1861), born in Brandon, a leading Illinois politician, opponent of total abolition of slavery. He was the regular Democratic candidate for President against Lincoln in 1860.

HENRY STEVENS (1819–1886), bookseller and scholar, was born at Barnet and always signed himself "G.M.B." (Green Mountain Boy) although he spent most of his life selling priceless books in England.

ADMIRAL GEORGE DEWEY (1837–1917), the great hero of the Spanish-American War, and victor at Manila Bay, where he destroyed the entire Spanish fleet without losing a single man. Born at Montpelier.

CHESTER A. ARTHUR (1830–1886), born in Fairfield, became by the assassination of Garfield the 21st President of the United States. He dismayed the politicians by becoming an honest, effective President.

CALVIN COOLIDGE (1872–1933), born at Plymouth, became 30th President of the United States on the death of Warren Harding. "Coolidge prosperity" was the popular name for one of America's wildest booms.

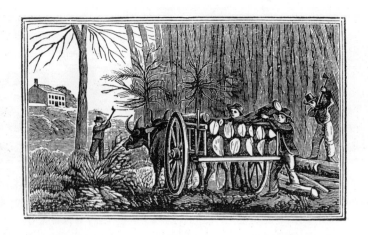

Green Mountain Life

If the artists of a hundred years ago neglected the prettiest and oldest towns, so that we cannot know just how Windsor, Arlington, or Bradford looked, they have done better for the daily life and work of their time. Besides, Vermonters still do many of the old things, sometimes even in the old way. Walter Needham of modern Guilford has told how he learned from his grandfather to work slate, lay stone walls, brew Indian herb medicines, and make anything he wanted by going into the woods for it. His grandfather's ways were the usual ones in Vermont up to perhaps 1900, as they had been in western Massachusetts fifty years earlier, and in Connecticut around 1800. Naturally pioneer life moved along with the frontier.

The Vermont countryside has about it that which will give it forever a touch of the frontier. You may not use ox power (though some Vermonters still do), but usually the best way to cut wood is to take an axe and cut it, as the men at the head of this page did when my great-grandfather was a boy in Rutland. Maple syrup has gone from black to palest amber well within living memory, but this is only by doing more carefully just what the people in Rowland Robinson's novels did. You still have to tap the trees just so, and you still tremble at every change in the sky. Being fussy enough to strain out the twigs and skim off the froth and watch a thermometer is no great matter, after all.

Not all the early Vermonters were pious churchgoers. True, the settlers in the Connecticut Valley were mostly stout Congregationalists, one of whose first acts was to knock together a house of worship like the one at the left; before long they would advance to the framed meeting house at the right, and woe betide the reprobate who shirked meeting. But the western slope was another matter. Said our friend the Reverend Perkins in 1789, "About 1–2 would be glad to have ye Gospel & to support public worship. The rest would chuse to have no Sabbath no ministers — no religion — no heaven — no hell — no morality."

I have already said that early Vermont cherished her hard-earned schools, but even in Vermont it was nice when school let out.

School life was just as rugged as life in the woods or behind the plow. You huddled around a stove, "scorched in front and froze behind," and were lucky if the ink didn't freeze in your pen even so.

Your pen was a goose quill. "The complaint of having wretched pens is a plea that ought never to be accepted from a young lady.

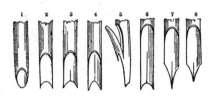

Quills are easily obtained, and she ought to be able to make or mend a pen herself. She should be furnished with a good penknife." The cut shows how.

Below is one of the century-old schools of Vermont, Burr Seminary in Manchester. It opened in 1833, with an endowment willed by Joseph Burr, who had "accumulated property by patient industry and an upright course of business." There were 146 students the first term, most of them candidates for the gospel ministry. "Its situation among the Green Mountains is pleasant, retired and healthful, and where there are few temptations to extravagance and vice."

Below is the original building of the University of Vermont,

established at Burlington partly by the urging of Ira Allen. The first Commencement was in 1804. During the War of 1812 Army occupation "destroyed the fences and very much interrupted the collegiate exercises."

Down to 22 students and faced with suspension in 1821, the University made a strong recovery, and has since become nationally eminent.

"The scenery about Burlington is romantic. The dome of the University is the best place from which to obtain a good view of the surrounding country."

Middlebury College, as we have already seen, owed its beginning partly to Timothy Dwight, who happened to be at Middlebury in 1798, and was impatient with the delay in launching the University.

The buildings of Norwich University burned in 1866, six years after this picture recorded them. The school was moved to Northfield, which had just lost its railroad offices to St. Albans.

Leland and Gray Seminary in Townshend has also had its fires, but it still instructs the young people of the West River Valley at the old stand, as it has been doing since 1834.

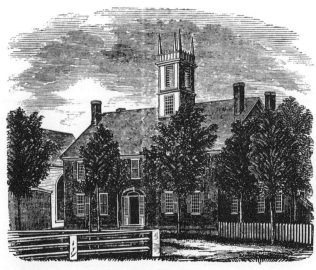

HOLBROOK

43

The fact that Vermont is an impregnable Republican stronghold does not mean that Vermonters cannot be excited about politics. Torchlight processions like this one were a favorite amusement around election time in your grandfather's youth.

But torchlight processions were too mild to let off the steam of one Vermont excitement that completely mystifies us today. From 1826 to 1836 the great political issue here was "anti-Masonry." A renegade York State Freemason disappeared, and the Freemasons were accused of murdering him. For ten years, denouncing the Freemasons was almost enough of itself to get you elected in Vermont; such papers as the Woodstock *American Whig*, *Vermont Luminary and Equal Rights* filled their columns with nothing else.

Another movement that swept the Green Mountains we can understand much better, though it is hard for us to take in the conditions that brought it about. You may not even realize, without being told, that the Fatal Ladder so vividly depicted at the right goes down rung by rung from a sociable swig of hard cider to beastly drunkenness. And I do not print the picture merely to be funny. Listen to a keen observer in the Connecticut Valley of the 1830s: "The greatest vice I knew was drunkenness. The rum-bottle stood upon the sideboard, and a cider-barrel was always on tap in the cellar. Whoever

called, if only the next neighbor to borrow a hoe or a shovel, was offered a bowl of apples and a mug of cider, if not something stronger. The ordinary spirits, New England rum, whiskey, and cider-brandy, cost from fifteen to twenty-five cents a gallon. Everybody asked everybody to drink. The man who went up to a bar asked his acquaintance to drink with him: and he invited all present, whether he knew them or not, if he wished to be considered a

good fellow. There were drunken lawyers, drunken doctors, drunken members of Congress, drunken ministers.

"A reaction came; when people, in order to be temperate, refused to drink even a glass of cider, the farmers cut down their great, beautiful orchards."

The newly reformed drunkard at the left is welcoming a cup of cold water on a hot day.

45

Life in Vermont, as anywhere else, is made up much more of many small excitements than of a few big ones. Each season in the year brings its own duties and pleasures; and the Green Mountains are governed by the seasons beyond anything that a city-dweller to southward can imagine. Above you see one of the many delights of early winter, before the snow spoils the ice. A century has done little to change this picture, beyond shortening skirts.

At the left, however, is the disastrous result of ignoring your older brother when he says the ice is still too thin.

Vermont still has its sleighs — one jingles past my house every winter morning, taking the teacher to the district school —, but hardly enough, alas, to make such races as the one below a common sight. "The sleigh-rides!" a Yankee, T. L. Nichols, explained to the British, "The snow is four feet deep, but trodden in the road-way hard as rock. You glide along swiftly to the music of the jingling bells, just feeling the motion, and wrapped in buffalo robes. Fancy a line of twenty sleighs, with as many loving couples, gliding through the frozen landscape by moonlight."

The event at the right took place "in the northern part of Vermont. The two boys had occasion to pass through a dense forest for four miles. They were startled at the gruff bark of a wolf." In fact there were two, and the boys escaped only by the sleigh's overturning and covering them.

Being spilled into the snow was a jolly mishap by comparison.

Below is a scene in the general store at West Rutland a little later in the year. The local boys passed spare moments of the sugar season with "French wrestling."

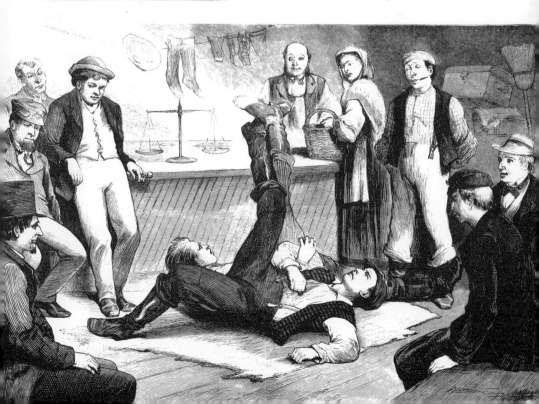

People who have never been in Vermont naturally suppose that you have to stay indoors in winter; whereas actually, of course, you get much of your work done when the snow will bear you. Winter is when you need firewood, and winter is when you get it, as these boys are doing.

At other seasons you might get out the old bucksaw, with its thong stretcher, and saw the wood into stove lengths.

One vanished occupation is raising flax and weaving linen at home. Flax-breakers like the one at the left are now curiosities found in sheds. Once linen was the common wear; anything really grand was "as fine as a cotton shirt."

48

 The sugar maple has become the trademark of Vermont, though all the northern states once depended on maple sugar for their every-day sweetening. White sugar, not maple, was the holiday treat that crusty old country store-keepers did not carry because it sold out too fast. Old books used to estimate how important the sugar crop was to the prosperity of Vermont, figuring it at ten cents a pound. Nowadays our syrup is so clear that "Yorkers" complain it can't be real maple, but must have cane in it.

It is, just the same, though lean-tos, kettles, and sap yokes have yielded to sugarhouses, evaporators (not so primitive now as the one below), and gathering-tanks. No amount of modern improvements will make the sap run unless you have snow on the ground, freezing nights, and warm days. It still takes a barrel of sap to make a single gallon of syrup, and you are still very lucky if the run lasts a month.

Sugar used to be preferred to syrup because it was easier to store.

When the sugar-boilers get hungry, said a magazine of 1850, "as people are pretty apt to do on occasions like this, a slice of brown bread, thickly covered with half-boiled sap, forms a very satisfying luncheon."

Every step in sugaring is fun, but the big jollification (above) comes at the end of the season. "The farmers take turns in inviting their neighbors to a sugaring-off, when the most interesting and fascinating of the population gather around the boiling sweetness and make merry while the hours slip away. It is estimated that the sugar-making season does more to encourage marriage than almost any other industrial phenomenon in nature."

When the frost come out of the ground, you build fences.

PEEP-FROG

Need I tell you that this is spring? Hard upon sugaring come mud-time and plowing; no progress can change that.

Indeed progress has gone backward, for many a Vermont motorist has had to send for horses to draw him out of the mud.

By the time the mud dries up a little, you are ready to sow.

Once upon a time all Vermont was busy shearing its sheep in June. In 1840 Vermont had almost six sheep for each one human inhabitant, and Vermont Merino sheep were as famous as Vermont maple syrup is now. In just the same way, too, sheep would be smuggled in from New Hampshire and New York, and then sold as the genuine Vermont product.

The saying was that Nature had sharpened the noses of sheep until they could find grass even among the rocks of Vermont. Between 1811 and 1846 Vermont became more and more one vast sheep run. It was in 1811 that William Jarvis brought to Weathersfield the fine Spanish Merino flock he had bought in Spain when the Napoleonic wars broke down the old strict embargo.

For about twenty years the whole prosperity of the state rested on sheep, first on wool, then on breeding stock for sale to other parts of the country. Big sheep farmers bought out small farmers to get pasture, and so the population of Vermont shrank as the sheep increased. But first the removal of the high tariff on wool, and then western competition, killed the business.

These prize ewes were raised at Westminster.

52

The famous Morgan horse that trots uphill and walks down is another son of the Green Mountains. The sire of the strain came to Randolph in 1795. By 1831 a schoolbook said, "The horses are very fine ones. Many of the fine horses you see in New York, Boston, and Hartford, come from Vermont."

The magazine editor who printed this picture did not seem sure whether the young lady was the farmer's daughter or a summer visitor; at any rate she is on her way to celebrate the height of summer by helping get the hay in.

The next page is a whole vista of summer and fall. A man mowing with the old-fashioned kind of scythe and cradle that can be found rusting in most Vermont barns is the first figure. Next comes the wheat harvest. The Vermont pioneers who settled on the very tops of the hills grew almost nothing but wheat, though after they moved down to the valleys a wheat blight and the competition of the western prairies drove the farmers to other crops. The people with the cart are going out to pick peaches. Peaches are hard to grow as far north as the Green Mountains, but if they will grow at all they are the very best. The same thing is true of apples. Corn took the place of wheat as the chief grain crop in Vermont, and your neighbor today will sell you delicious sweet corn. What Vermont child does not look forward to the butternut season? And butternut dye gave homespun its special color. Then there is a cider mill, and finally a husking bee with the cider going round.

54

CRADLING

WHEAT HARVEST

GOING PEACH-PICKING

APPLES ARE RIPE

CUTTING CORN

NUT-GATHERING

CIDER PRESS

HUSKING FROLIC

Spreading manure and threshing are winter tasks, and so is winnowing. The happy reunion at the right, Vermonters will not need to be told, is town exiles home for Thanksgiving.

"The Thanksgiving dinner forms a prominent feature of the picture. Every farmer's table now literally groans with the weight of the feast; the delicious pumpkin pie leads a host of other dainties in the bountiful dessert." The feasters below thoughtfully allow us a glimpse of the brick oven next the fireplace, where all the baking was done before the time of Conant and his stoves.

Until railroads changed things, December brought every Vermont farmer to the grist mill with a load of grain. Present-day Weston has a mill going again.

The great pine forests of New England are gone, even from inexhaustible Maine; yet Vermonters to this day are handy with an axe, and have a way with wood. Go up into the mountains along any fair-sized stream, and you may look for a sawmill, though it will not be an up-and-down mill like the one above, which sawed so slowly that you could put on a log and go home for dinner. A neighbor of mine has a mill that makes cider in fall, and lumber when he needs it the rest of the time.

Woodworking industries of all kinds still thrive in Vermont. They have made up in variety what they may have lost in size. In addition to sawmills, cooper shops (below) were perhaps likely to be the biggest establishments in the days when maple sugar, butter, and nearly everything else came in a tub or bucket. (That was one reason why the farmers made sugar, instead of syrup — it was much easier to store in a home-made tub. You had to have a jug from the store to keep syrup in.)

"Manufactures," says a gazetteer, "flourish on many of the delightful streams of Vermont. The scenery of this state is very romantic and beautiful; the air is pure and healthful; the people industrious, intelligent, hospitable."

Most of the industries in early Vermont started before there were any factories. Either people spun and wove their own cloth, for instance, or a neighbor did it for them. The family at left are carding, spinning, and weaving wool; probably they were the neighborhood weavers, too, and wove yarn other housewives had spun.

The shoemaker, on the other hand, traveled around with his tools and hides from farm to farm. He would stay several days at each place, until he had supplied the whole family with enough cowhide boots to last a year or two. They were uncomfortable, but they wore forever.

The carriage builder and the wheelwright were as

Perhaps nobody is so important now as the blacksmith used to be. He was about the only man from whom every farmer had to buy; he did all the business of a modern garage, machine shop, and hardware store. The smith was a mighty man indeed.

important in Vermont villages then as the garage is nowadays.

For such a rough and snowy state, Vermont has produced a lot of sweetness — maple in spring, honey in summer. Bee-keeping has followed the buck-wheat crop around the state, but you have always been able to find good honey somewhere in the Green Mountains.

Now we come to the Vermont industries that need a real factory.

Platform scales, as we have already seen, are an old Vermont specialty. Thaddeus Fairbanks of St. Johnsbury invented the modern kind, for which he was knighted by the Emperor of Austria, besides making all Caledonia County prosperous. Howe of Rutland is another great scale maker.

For many years "Bennington" and "pottery" went together just like "maple" and "sugar." The Norton family began making sturdy jugs and housewares there in 1793, and in the mid-nineteenth century Christopher Fenton introduced his much-sought-after "Parian" porcelain.

Nowadays the very name of Vermont calls up images of a general store like the famous one at Williamsville, which carries everything from pulpits on down. Yet the eighteenth century was nearly over before we could boast of a single store; and then the stock was probably little more than salt, tea, and rum. The storekeeper took most of his pay in trade, as some do today. Drygoods stores like this one reached Vermont well along in the 19th century.

Even after general stores came in, lots of remote hill farms were too far away. So they depended for news and "Yankeee notions" on tin-peddlers who toiled along the rutted cart tracks with wagon-loads of kitchenware, needles, thread, clocks, ribbons, shawls. Jim Fisk got his start as a Vermont tin-peddler, and within just a few years he was a partner in the great Boston drygoods house of Jordan Marsh.

Vermont has so much stone and such shrewd traders that they can dig up the stone and sell it to softer climates and people. Below at the left is a marble quarry; Vermont produces even more granite than the Granite State; roofing slate, which now comes from Poultney and Fair Haven, was first quarried in Guilford.

"The scenery along the banks of the Connecticut is exceedingly varied and picturesque, and though many of the streams surpass it in grandeur of features, yet for the variety, elegance and cheerfulness of the landscape which its borders everywhere  exhibit, it may be regarded as one of the most beautiful rivers in the world. Its waters afford vast numbers of the finest shad, and

the taking of these fish furnishes occupation to many of the inhabitants along the river."

The man who lived in the homestead on the hill probably thought little of the covered bridge, and he may have been pleased with the convenience of the railroad, if it didn't frighten his cows too badly. Now the covered bridge has become an antiquity, though Vermont

 still has more than its share, some of them the latticed structures for which Nicholas M. Powers of Pittsford was famous. He built them all over Vermont and New Hampshire, leaving a stronger mark on the countryside than his more internationally celebrated namesake Hiram Powers did with his statuary.

61

Vermont life indoors has been pretty much the same as that in the rest of back-country New England — the dairy with its earthen milk pans, its probably home-made wooden buckets, its neck-yoke to lighten the task of carrying two heavy pails, its dasher churn (in dairying Vermont, milk often flowed more freely than water in the kitchen, unless the house was lucky enough to have a spring up the hill); the pantry, full of good things protected (by the late date of this picture) with domed wire covers that are now rapidly becoming antique in their turn; the parlor, too seldom used even to be pictured by artists before the daguerreotype age, concerned rather with life than with funeral pomp. All of these scenes, naturally, are late and

luxurious if you compare them with the log-cabin Vermont of the Reverend Perkins' day. "When I go from hut to hut, from town to town, in y^e Wilderness, y^e people nothing to eat, — to drink, — or wear, — all work, & yet y^e women quiet, — serene, — peaceable, — contented. They set much more by one another than in y^e old settlements. Leave their doors unbarred."

This boy wishing he need not study is in one of the separate little offices that village lawyers used to have.

Said John Graham, of Rutland, in 1797, "The women of this State bear hardships to an incredible degree, and I must, in justice to my fair Countrywomen declare, that better housewives, or more expert in the use of the needle,

do not exist; nor do they confine themselves slothfully within doors when the labours of the field stand in need of their assistance, they then with chearfulness and alacrity join the men, and help to gather in the harvest. Then fathers, husbands, wives, children, unite with one accord."

Perkins had taken a somewhat gloomier view: "I grieve to hear what thousands & thousands have endured — women & children in coming to this State of Vermont. I ask myself are these women of y^e same species with our fine Ladies? tough are they, brawny their limbs, — their young girls

unpolished — & will bear work as well as mules. People nasty — poor — low-lived — indelicate — and miserable cooks. Many, profane — yet cheerful & much more contented than in Hartford—and the women more contented than ye men — turned tawny by ye smoke of ye log-huts."

We have come to the end of our Vermont journey through space and time. It might have been longer if Vermonters had been more self-conscious; but that is a quality the Green Mountains do not allow. Only after thirty-five years did Seth Hubbell of Wolcott find time to describe his settling: "I had now got to the end of my journey, and I may say almost to the end of my property, for I had not a mouthful of meat or kernel of grain for my family, nor had I a cent of money left to buy with. I however had the good luck to catch a saple. The skin I carried fifty miles, and exchanged for half a bushel of wheat, and backed it home. We had now lived three weeks without bread; though in the time I had bought a moose of an Indian, and backed the meat five miles. No grain or provision of any kind, of consequence, was to be had on the river Lamoille. I had to go into New Hampshire, sixty miles, for the little I had for my family, till harvest, and this was so scanty a pittance that we were under the painful necessity of allowancing the children till we had a supply. The three remaining children that I left in Hydepark, I brought one at a time on my back on snow-shoes, as also the whole of my goods. When I came into Wolcott, my farming tools consisted of one axe and an old hoe. The first year I cleared about two acres, wholly without any team."

Until such a man — or more likely his son — could look out cozily from a warm fire through glass windows to his own snowy hillsides, he would not waste much time telling the story, let alone drawing pictures of the scene.